ALN

THE PICKLING HANDBOOK

© Bokforlaget Max Ström
Original title: Syra själv. Konsten att förädla grönsaker med hälsosamma bakterier
Original ISBN: 978-91-7126-253-0

Text Karin Bojs
Photography Per Ranung
Design Mikael Engblom
Recipe testing Anna Sjögren
Illustration p. 109 Mattias Abrahamsson

© for the English edition: h.f.ullmann publishing GmbH

Translation from Swedish: Malcolm Garrard for JMS Books (www.jmseditorial.com)
Project management for h.f.ullmann: Lars Pietzschmann

Overall responsibility for production: h.f.ullmann publishing GmbH, Potsdam, Germany

Printed in Italy, 2014

ISBN 978-3-8480-0678-6

10 9 8 7 6 5 4 3 2 1
X IX VIII VII VI V IV III II I

www.ullmann-publishing.com
newsletter@ullmann-publishing.com
facebook.com/ullmann.social

KARIN BOJS

THE PICKLING HANDBOOK

HOMEMADE RECIPES TO ENJOY YEAR-ROUND

PHOTOGRAPHY PER RANUNG

*h.f.*ullmann

CONTENTS

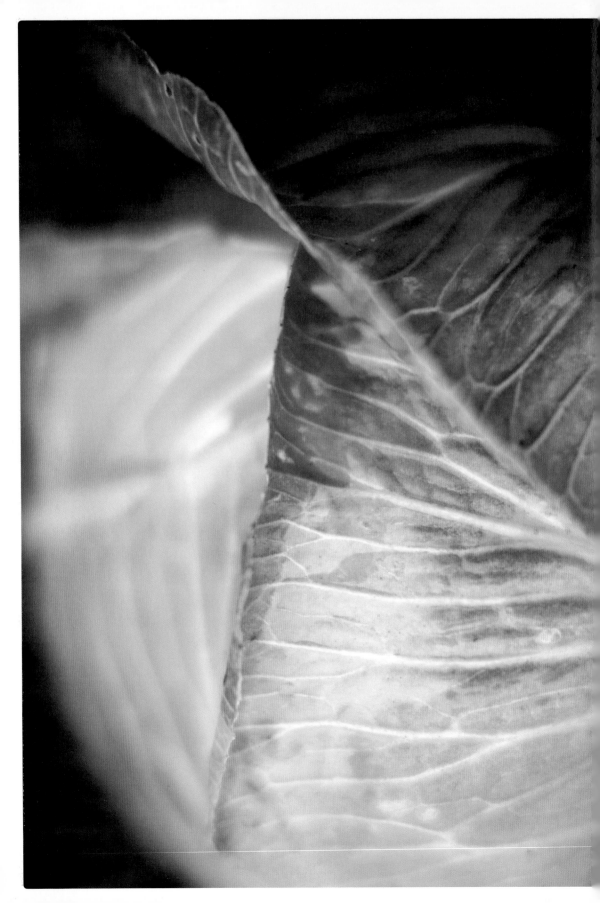

INTRODUCTION

As fall gives way to winter, my refrigerator fills up with colorful jars. There are slices of carrot, brilliant orange and sharp as sour candies, and olive-green pickles that are supremely tasty with a dab of honey and sour cream. There are pink onions, dazzling white sauerkraut, and, most beautiful of all, red cabbage, whose deep purple color reminds me of a fine wine.

Pickling vegetables has become a hobby of mine, and I now regard winter as one of the best food seasons of the year, as this is when the contents of my jars are ready to eat. It is time to break out tangy crudités for weekday lunches, serve my dinner guests choucroute, and show off my best sour beet salad with walnuts.

The pickling itself can be made into an event, as it was way back when we all lived off the land; in fact, as people still do in Switzerland, in the Gürbe Valley—known as "Cabbage Land"—where sauerkraut traditions still run deep. Here, they get together, drink wine, tread sauerkraut, and listen to groups of yodelers; on a trip with Eldrimner, the National Swedish Center for Artisan Food, I was privileged to attend one of these gatherings in the company of several of Sweden's foremost pickling experts.

Lacto-fermentation is one of the oldest and simplest methods of conserving and refining food known to man. It is low-energy and low-tech, and brings out subtle and complex flavors that can't be achieved with quicker methods.

In other words, it's an art that's due a renaissance.

I have written this book because I want to share my pickling experiences. I have had a deep interest in food since my early teens: I studied food technology in school and spent the following decade working in fine bakeries and patisseries in Gothenburg. I think it is important that food tastes good, of course, but I'm also fascinated by the processes—biological and chemical—that turn raw ingredients into edible produce.

After a while, my scientific interests began to take over: I gained some more qualifications and I have been the Science Editor for the Swedish newspaper *Dagens Nyheter* for the past 15 years. My day-to-day work covers state-of-the-art research from all over the world and my articles can be about anything from climate change to the latest methods of DNA-mapping; however, the connection between this cutting-edge technology and sauerkraut isn't actually as far-fetched as one might think.

Covering environmental and health matters has opened my eyes to what is missing from our modern lifestyle. Many of these problems can only be solved on a large scale, of course, through political, economic, and technological measures, but an individual's personal choices can also make a difference. I have tried to clean up my own life and move in a more climate-friendly and healthy direction, and growing and pickling vegetables fit in well with this ambition.

Recent DNA research has given us insights into the workings of the human intestine that were previously unimaginable. Thanks to this, we are finding answers to a whole range of questions about what actually happens during lacto-fermentation and how lactic acid bacteria affect our health.

Pickling is a venerable and traditional technique and there is a wealth of knowledge to be found in the old practices—but with tradition comes myth, and the world of pickling is filled with baseless rumors and unsubstantiated claims.

My approach comes from domestic pickling—the practical experience I have acquired at home in my kitchen—but I am also a science journalist, weighing up all the information, tracking down the best analyses, and consulting leading researchers, so there are no old wives' tales in this book, just well-documented facts.

KARIN BOJS

1. GETTING STARTED

Lactic acid bacteria are living organisms, just like you or me, and have certain basic requirements for life. While their needs are essentially pretty modest—which is what makes pickling so easy and safe—the bacteria do need nourishment (as well as sufficient water and salt) and a warm environment, and there must be no harmful substances present to poison them. If you can satisfy these few requirements, lactic acid bacteria will grow and flourish, driving out any unwanted microorganisms that might spoil the food and harm you.

SUGAR

The most important nutrient for lactic acid bacteria is sugar. If the sugar content is too low, your pickling will fail, so it is important to select vegetables that are of good quality and—in the case of cucumber and cabbage, at least—freshly picked. The moment a cucumber or cabbage is taken from the plant, the sugars start to degrade, and things then go downhill rapidly. For cucumbers, pickling a couple of days after being harvested might already be too late, for cabbages a couple of months, so it is best to coordinate pickling with the picking seasons. There is an optimum season for every vegetable— see Chapter 2 for more information.

It is also crucial that crops destined for pickling have enough sun and nutrients while growing, an important point to remember for those who grow their own vegetables.

Some vegetables don't contain enough sugar to be pickled in isolation; this is the case with beans and mushrooms, for example, so they should be mixed with produce with a high sugar content, such as onions. This is explained in the recipe section of the book.

BRINE: A SALT AND WATER SOLUTION

Lactic acid bacteria prefer to live in water, rather than air, which brings us to the most common mistake made by home picklers: when vegetables are exposed to the air, other—uninvited—microorganisms will immediately hijack the pickling process. It is crucial to tread cabbage, for example, until it releases its juices and then to press it down into the pickling jar so that any

Lactic acid bacteria need sugar as a nutrient. Root vegetables such as carrots, parsnips, and rutabagas are a rich source of sugar.

air bubbles are released. It is essential to make sure that cucumber, carrots, and beets are completely covered with brine, and don't forget to check the brine levels at regular intervals—if the liquid reduces by too much, make some more brine and top it off.

There are several methods for ensuring the liquid in the jar is retained and preventing it from evaporating, but the essential point to remember is that the lid should not be completely tight: lactic acid bacteria create carbon dioxide gas at the start of the pickling process, and this must be allowed to escape.

Traditional ceramic pickling jars are cleverly constructed for this exact purpose, with a groove in their top rims that is filled with water before the lid is put on. The water stops air from entering the vessel but allows excess carbon dioxide to escape; this type of jar also comes with special ceramic weights to push the pickled product down into the brine.

A simpler and more old-fashioned method is to use a wooden barrel or a ceramic jar. Press the pickles down with a plate, then weigh the plate down with a large, clean stone (note that the stone must be very well washed—you could even boil it to sterilize it—and don't use limestone, which would react with the acid).

These methods all have their own particular aesthetic, cultural, and historic appeal, but I recommend an easier approach—use standard glass preserving jars. You can buy these in most kitchenware stores or order them online or by mail order. The jars come with a rubber seal that is placed inside the lid—don't forget this, or the air will be able to escape.

Instead of using the old stone method, you can press the vegetables down into the pickling liquid in one of the following ways:

1. Pour some water into a plastic bag, press out all the air, and seal it. You now have a small, flexible water cushion that can be placed in the top of the jar. Make sure it is big enough and really covers the pickle. This is more or less what many industrial sauerkraut manufacturers do, although they use cushions that are specially made from heavy-duty plastic.
2. Buy standard plastic containers that you would normally use for freezing food. Cut out disks from the plastic, ensuring they are the correct size to

Glass preserving jars with a rubber seal work just as well as traditional ceramic jars.

fit inside your preserving jars, and press them down onto the vegetables using small glass jars. Start collecting jars of varying sizes so that you can adjust to the correct size for your needs.

In both cases it is important to make sure that the plastic is approved for use with food.

SALT

Lactic acid bacteria prefer a salt content of between 1.5 percent and 2.2 percent, but, as they are such modest and tolerant creatures, anything between 0.5 percent and 3 percent may work, if you are lucky. I would recommend that you are as accurate as possible, and calculate the correct amount of salt and weigh out your vegetables and salt rather than chancing it.

The salt should be iodine-free, for reasons that are explained below. For pickling cabbage, the salt should also be fine-grain, so that it dissolves quickly and a salt level is achieved in which the lactic acid bacteria (but no uninvited microorganisms) can thrive as soon as possible.

You can also use brine for cucumbers, carrots, beet, beans, and many other vegetables. Note that the finished product should have a salt content of roughly 1.5 percent; the vegetables themselves contain minute amounts of salt, so the amount of salt in the brine needs to be higher than this. Prepare the brine shortly before you start pickling by boiling the water and mixing in your measured quantity of salt. Boiling the water isn't strictly necessary, but it is more hygienic and it also helps the salt to dissolve more quickly. Remember to make sure that the brine has cooled to room temperature before you use it.

TEMPERATURE

The ideal temperature for lacto-fermentation is around 59–64.4°F/15–18°C, but the bacteria aren't especially fussy, even here. Most professional cabbage-picklers don't regulate their pickling temperatures throughout the season, from late summer, when the temperature can rise considerably, to late fall, when it drops to not far above freezing. In hotter temperatures, fermentation speeds up, and pickles become more sour with a flatter taste and won't keep so long. When the weather is cooler, fermentation slows down and the flavors become more complex. If it is too cold, however, the fermentation process won't start at all.

The small batches of pickles that you make in your kitchen at home are more sensitive to variations in heat, so try to keep to the temperatures recommended in the recipes; this is especially important with cabbage, as it tends to ferment in two stages. During the first 24 hours, 68–71.6°F/20–22°C is best and it is easy to heat a room to this level, but after that you should lower the temperature to around 59°F/15°C, which can be tricky to achieve in modern homes. In our house, we put a thermometer in the cellar and once the temperature has dropped to 59°F/15°C, we start the cabbage. This usually occurs at the end of October. Once the produce is pickled, it will need to mature and should be kept refrigerated. But what if you've pickled so much that your refrigerator isn't big enough? A cool cellar is an ideal storage place if you're lucky enough to have one; another alternative is a well-insulated container on a balcony, which will work nicely if the winter doesn't get too harsh.

TOXINS

No harmful materials should be allowed to contaminate the lactic acid bacteria, and you will need to protect them from several modern-day household substances:

Iodine. Common household salt is enriched with iodine. This is great for humans, as it protects us from iodine deficiency, but it is bad for microorganisms as iodine has antibacterial properties. Always use iodine-free salt for pickling.

Chlorine. Water treatment plants often add chlorine to drinking water for the precise purpose of killing bacteria. But living bacteria is needed for pickling, so bring the water you're going to use to a boil and let it stand for an hour so, and the chlorine will evaporate.

Dish soap. Lactic acid bacteria can be harmed by traces of dishwashing liquid, so always make sure that jars and other equipment are well rinsed.

Acid. It might sound counterintuitive, but there is only so much acid a lactic acid bacterium can take. This is why most berries and fruits cannot be pickled—they are simply too acidic to start with—and it is also why the fermentation process eventually stops. More information about pH levels and the different kinds of lactic acid bacteria can be found in Chapter 6.

HYGIENE

Good hygiene is essential for lactic bacteria to get off to a good start without competition from other microorganisms, which, in a worst-case scenario, could also make you very ill. Vegetables must be scrubbed clean of any soil—if you are growing your own, mulch the soil beneath the vegetable crop with grass cuttings or sheets of newspaper to minimize contact with the earth. Wash and rinse the jars you use thoroughly.

ORGANIC: YES OR NO?

There are many advantages to buying organic produce; you are contributing to the health of the environment—and that of the farmer—but for pickling, it doesn't really matter if the vegetables you buy are produced organically or conventionally, and I have visited commercial sauerkraut manufacturers that run organic and conventional production operations in tandem. The main thing is that the vegetables are of good quality and are fresh and free from soil or any wilted parts.

For making sourdough bread, however, it is important to choose organic flour, as certain molds that exist in the grain are key. If grain is sourced from wheat and rye fields that are sprayed to combat mold when farmed conventionally, these molds can be killed.

BACTERIA: THEIR JOURNEY

Lactic acid bacteria occur naturally on all plants, so your job is merely to make sure they thrive, reproduce, and are able to fight off competition from other microorganisms. This is achieved by maintaining an appropriate temperature and providing an oxygen-free environment with sufficient levels of salt: the lactic acid bacteria will soon take over, even though they may only make up a thousandth of the plant's bacteria flora to begin with. If you provide the right conditions, different types of lactic acid bacteria will succeed one another during the pickling process, producing tasty pickles that will keep. There is no need to add a culture at the start of the process. See Chapter 6 for more information.

Good hygiene is essential—scrub vegetables to remove all traces of soil.

EQUIPMENT

The equipment required to start pickling should be found in most kitchens already: a set of measuring spoons and ideally a set of scales, a saucepan to boil the brine in, a thermometer, plastic bags, a cutting board, a knife, and glass preserving jars with rubber seals. A mandoline is handy if you're going to use thin slices of carrot, beet, or cabbage. Food processors work for carrots, beet, and so on, but they can be a bit impractical for cabbage as you have to cut the cabbage head into thin wedges to get it into the machine's feeder tube. Traditional wooden tools for shredding cabbage are wonderfully clever and extremely useful. If you're thinking of buying only one new piece of equipment for your new pickling hobby, I recommend a kraut board: they are available by mail order and are relatively inexpensive.

You don't really need to buy specially made ceramic pickling jars, which are big and tricky to fit into a modern refrigerator. They are also impractical, in the sense that they have such a large capacity—holding much more than the average family can get through in a couple of weeks. And every time you take out some pickle, you let oxygen into the jar, which speeds up decay. Glass preserving jars in more useful sizes are more practical.

You can also buy special wooden cabbage beaters, but although attractive and inexpensive, they are not really necessary. It is important to tread the cabbage thoroughly so it starts releasing its juices and all the air bubbles are pressed out, but you can just as easily use your fists for smaller batches. I recommend using your feet—well washed of course—for larger batches; almost all professional cabbage picklers I have seen use their feet, wearing appropriate and exceptionally clean boots, of course.

Is your kitchen equipment ready? It's time for the vegetables to take center stage!

......

A traditionally made "kraut board" is an extremely useful tool. More modern equipment, such as a plastic mandoline, also works well. Keep the blades sharp.

2. THE CYCLE OF THE SEASONS

Lacto-fermentation is a food preservation method that is all about harnessing nutrients and tastes. Preserving food allows those of us who live in temperate climes to make the best of every season. Such knowledge has often been neglected in these modern times of imported food and unlimited access to freezers, but we are now becoming more aware of the importance of the annual seasonal cycle. This is good news both environmentally and gastronomically, as our diet becomes tastier and more varied.

SUMMER

Looking after the cucumber patch is one of my favorite summer pastimes. It is only about 1 square yard (1 square meter) in size, but it provides me with lovely cucumbers from the middle of July until the first frost. I pick the small, round fruit a couple of times a week and, at the same time, I take the opportunity to cut some sprigs of dill and a couple of black currant leaves. Back in the kitchen, I wash the cucumbers and prick them with a sharp knife, before throwing them all in a preserving jar and covering them with brine. Once you have established your own method and routine, it only takes a couple of minutes. The result is like a bright-green painting—an intense splash of chlorophyll, like summer captured in a jar. The emerald color soon starts to fade to olive-green, but the cucumbers just get tastier and are ready in a couple of weeks. We can sit in our rose garden and feast on our first pickles in early August. This coincides nicely with the season for freshly creamed honey, a delicious accompaniment to the cucumbers.

LATE SUMMER, EARLY FALL

The cucumbers are soon followed in August and September by a range of vegetables that are also good to pickle, either on their own or in a variety of combinations. These include:

String beans and green and yellow beans
Tomatoes (green and red)
Zucchini and other summer squashes
Cauliflower
Bell peppers
Chile peppers
Shallots
Garlic, garlic tops or stems

Small, crunchy cauliflower heads turn into a real delicacy when served with winter crudités, and pickled red tomatoes beat any ketchup you can buy. Pickled shallots are much tastier than onions that have been pickled with sugar. You can even pickle beans and mushrooms, but you have to weigh up the work involved and the taste that it is possible to achieve against other methods of preservation, such as freezing, salting, drying, and the hermetic sealing of boiled vegetables.

FALL

Late October or early November is when you can enjoy a great sauerkraut extravaganza. This is when the cabbage is ripe, the sugar content is at its highest, and storage space in your cellar is at an ideal temperature.

My mother-in-law, Linda, is Estonian-Swedish and grew up on a self-sufficient farm just outside the coastal town of Haapsalu in Estonia, in the Baltic region of Northern Europe. She has told me tales of her child-hood and how her father used to spend a whole day tending to the family's cabbage supplies for the year ahead. The children were allowed to try the sugary cabbage heads, and she can still remember how tasty they were—as sweet as apples.

A friend with Latvian roots recalls a festival called Talka, where people would gather together to harvest, shred, and pickle their cabbage. I was lucky enough to experience a similar event in Chabisland ("Cabbage Land") in Switzerland (*chabis* is the Swiss-German word for cabbage), where the Thurnen Sauerkraut company organizes a special day in the village of Mühlethurnen in celebration of cabbage. People travel from far and wide, bringing their traditional ceramic jars with them, and can even buy pre-shredded cabbage from Thurnen's factory, sparing them the most arduous part of the process. They are given small, pre-weighed bags of salt (with or without spices), and then, standing in long rows in an enormous factory hall, they get to work preparing the cabbage, pounding the shredded leaves with special wooden hammers, or squeezing it with their hands. There is a bar selling wine, and at lunchtime they enjoy sauerkraut with plentiful portions of sausage and pork. When I was there, the wine continued to flow and a family orchestra provided some entertainment. The wife played bass, the sons played accordion, and the husband yodeled; it sounded rather like the band in Disney's *Snow White & The Seven Dwarves*, but perhaps more authentic.

LATE FALL

There is no need to turn your attention to your crops of beets, carrots, turnips, and rutabagas until you have dealt with the cabbage. These root vegetables contain more fructose and sucrose than cabbage and can be stored for a couple of months before the sugar levels fall so low that there is any danger of unwanted lactic acid bacteria. There are frequent arguments in our home over which pickled root vegetables are the tastiest, and it is usually a close-run thing between carrots and beets. Rutabaga, with its high vitamin C content, can be combined with carrots. Pickled turnips are a popular product in Switzerland, however, where they often mix equal measurements of sauerkraut and turnips.

WINTER

Winter marks the high point of the pickling year, the culmination of hard work since the summer or, for those who grow their own produce, since early spring. I have a friend, a professor of medicine, who takes out his first jar of sauerkraut on Christmas Eve, but I personally prefer to celebrate Christmas with the world's best herring salad, the recipe for which is on page 82. We start almost every weekday meal from January until early summer with some pickled crudités, such as carrot slices. The beet salad on page 90 will impress even the fussiest of dinner guests and once even earned me praise from the secret circle of restaurant critics at *Dagens Nyheter*, one of Sweden's largest daily newspapers. A beet soup of eastern European origin known as borscht takes on a whole new depth of flavors and sophistication if you add some pickled beet (see page 93). Warming up some sauerkraut and sausage makes for a very tasty winter meal that can be ready in minutes, and you might even be ambitious enough to make the sausage yourself. It is not as easy to prepare, of course, but all the tastier for it. Add some extra meat and you have what the French call *choucroute garnie* (see page 85). Cheese fondue is another perfect dish to serve guests in February and March; its flavor is enhanced and it is easier to digest when combined with pickled vegetables, such as carrots, cucumbers, cauliflower, bell peppers, and onions.

A PICKLER'S PLANTING CALENDAR

The following is only a rough guide—you will need to adjust planting and harvesting times according to the climate in your area.

JANUARY
- Plan your planting beds. Purchase seeds, or order online or by mail order. Choose varieties that are good for pickling, such as the pickling cucumber Northern Pickling, carrots such as Chantenay and Imperator, and the late-blooming Holsteiner Platter cabbage.

APRIL
- Sow seeds for cabbage, red cabbage, and cauliflower indoors to start with. Then, where possible, transfer the seedlings to a greenhouse or a cold frame.
- Dig over and prepare the planting beds with a rake. Newspaper makes a good, cheap mulch to suppress weeds—cover the soil with sheets of newspaper, then cover the paper with a layer of shredded leaves or wood chips to weigh it down. You can plant right through the mulch and paper.

MAY
- Sow beet and cucumber seeds indoors.
- Sow zucchini seeds indoors, or outdoors when all risk of frost has passed.
- Weed the planting beds every week, ideally mulching with grass cuttings if you have not already laid a mulch.
- Plant out cabbages and cover them well with netting in order to protect against insects.
- Sow beans indoors.

JUNE
- Plant out cucumber and zucchini.
- Sow carrots, rutabagas, and turnips.
- Weed the planting beds every week.

JULY
- Start harvesting cucumbers.
- Sow black radish and napa cabbage outdoors, for kimchi.

- Feed (fertilize) cabbage plants from time to time. Fresh human urine can be used—a total of 5 quarts/5 liters per 1 square yard/0.8 square meter over the course of the entire growing season (see below). NB Urine should be applied to the soil not to the plant.
- Weed the planting beds every week, adding further mulch when needed.

AUGUST
- Continue to harvest cucumbers; start picking zucchini, beans, and cauliflowers.
- Feed (fertilize) cabbage plants and add mulch when necessary.
- Weed the planting beds at least once a week.

SEPTEMBER
- Continue to harvest cucumbers, zucchini, beans, and cauliflowers.
- Feed (fertilize) cabbage, but make sure you leave a month between the last application of urine (if using) and picking.
- Weed the planting beds at least once a week.
- Now remove the netting and enjoy your beautiful cabbage patch.

OCTOBER
- Harvest cabbage, beets, carrots, rutabagas, and turnips.

NOVEMBER
- Once everything has been harvested, it is time to clear and dig over the beds. Use a sharp spade and divide the work up over several days, if the prospect seems a little daunting.
- If the soil is heavy, add cow or horse manure as a fertilizer (it is better to fertilize light soil in spring). Cabbage and cucumber beds in particular will need a lot of nutrients.
- Weed and mulch carefully and you can skip the fall dig after a few years.

CROP ROTATION
If possible, use at least three beds for crop rotation. All root vegetables (kale, cabbage, cauliflower, black radish, rutabagas, turnips, radishes, etc.) should ideally be grown together, and then moved to another bed the following year to reduce the risk of pests and diseases. Ideally leave at least three years (preferably six) before you plant these crops in the same bed again.

3. PICKLING RECIPES

CUCUMBERS

If your cucumbers are fresh and of good quality, they should pickle well.

canning jar that can hold 2–3 quarts/2–3 liters
1 quart/1 liter water
2 tbsp/40 g iodine-free salt
2¼ lb/1 kg Kirby (pickling) cucumbers
2–4 sprigs dill
3–6 blackcurrant or raspberry leaves
peeled cloves of garlic, 1 tsp/7.5 g mustard seeds, 2 bay leaves, a few slices
   of thoroughly cleaned horseradish, to taste

1. Boil the water and add the salt. Let the brine cool to room temperature.
2. Clean the cucumbers thoroughly with a brush, removing any traces of soil. Discard any cucumbers that are soft or rotten.
3. Make little holes in the cucumbers with a toothpick or knife. Rinse the dill and the leaves.
4. Make layers of cucumber, dill, leaves, garlic, mustard seeds, spices, and any horseradish in the jar. Pour over the brine.
5. Check that the brine covers the cucumbers completely. If not, boil some more brine using about 1 tbsp/20 g of salt per 1 quart/1 liter of water, leave to cool, and pour over the cucumbers.
6. Push the cucumbers down into the brine. You could use a tightly sealed water-filled plastic bag or the weights from your traditional ceramic pickling jar, if you are using one.
7. Close the lid and let the jar stand at room temperature for about 2 weeks. Check at regular intervals that the cucumbers are still covered with brine.
8. After 2 weeks, the fermented cucumbers will be ready to eat. Once opened, keep in the refrigerator.

TIP: Increasing the salinity to 4 tbsp/80 g of salt per 1 quart/1 liter of water will ensure the cucumbers keep for longer. You may find a white film will develop on the cucumbers or at the bottom of the jar; this is a layer of yeast and is not harmful to eat.

BEANS

4 canning jars that can hold 2 cups/500 ml each
3⅓ cups/800 ml water + water for parboiling
about 2 tbsp/40 g iodine-free salt
2¼ lb/1 kg green beans or yellow or green string beans
7 oz/200 g onions (2 medium), peeled and finely chopped

1. Boil the water and add the salt. Let the brine cool to room temperature.
2. Wash and clean the beans before blanching them in batches in boiling water. Remove each batch of beans with a slotted spoon after 4 minutes (when they are parboiled), chill in cold water, and reserve in a bowl.
3. Divide the chopped onion equally between the jars.
4. Place the beans on top of the onion in the jars. Pack them in as tightly as possible.
5. Pour the cooled brine over the beans, making sure the liquid covers them completely. If there is not enough, boil some more brine, using 1 tbsp/ 20 g of salt per quart/liter of water. Leave the brine to cool then pour it over the beans.
6. Push the beans down into the brine—you could use a tightly sealed water-filled plastic bag—and close the lid.
7. Let the jars stand at room temperature for about 2 weeks. Check at regular intervals that the beans are properly covered with brine.
8. After 2 weeks, transfer them to the refrigerator—they are now ready to eat.

PICKLED BEANS AND CUCUMBERS

You can save space and effort by pickling cucumbers and beans in the same container. They will usually be ready to eat at about the same time.

3-quart/3-liter container
1 quart/1 liter water + water for parboiling
3 tbsp/60 g iodine-free salt
2¼ lb/1 kg beans
2¼ lb/1 kg Kirby (pickling) cucumbers
sprigs of dill, blackcurrant or raspberry leaves, peeled garlic cloves,
    mustard seeds, spices, to taste

1. Boil the water and add the salt. Let the brine cool.
2. Wash and clean the beans. Blanch them in batches in boiling water. Remove each batch of beans with a slotted spoon after 4 minutes (when they are parboiled), chill in cold water, and reserve in a bowl.
3. Clean the cucumbers thoroughly with a brush before pricking them all over with a toothpick or knife. Discard any cucumbers that are soft or rotten. Rinse the dill and leaves.
4. Layer the cucumbers, beans, leaves, dill, garlic, mustard seeds, and any spices in the container.
5. Pour the cooled brine into the container. If there is not enough liquid to cover the beans and cucumbers, boil some more brine, using 1 tbsp/20 g salt per quart/liter of water. Leave the brine to cool, then pour it over the vegetables.
6. Push the cucumbers and beans down into the brine—you could use a tightly sealed water-filled plastic bag—and close the lid.
7. Let the container stand at room temperature for about 2 weeks. Check the fluid level in the container regularly; if it drops, add more boiled and cooled brine.
8. The cucumbers and beans will be ready to eat after 2 weeks and should now be stored in the refrigerator.

....

Pierce the cucumbers before putting them in the brine.

ZUCCHINI

If you grow your own, you are likely to have a glut of zucchini when they are in season, which is around September; zucchini are usually cheaper in the stores at this time as well. Pickling is a great way to get the best out of this abundance.

2-quart/2-liter container
3⅓ cups/800 ml water
about 6 tsp/30 g iodine-free salt
4½ lb/2 kg zucchini (courgettes)

1. Boil the water and add 2 tsp/10 g salt. Let the brine cool.
2. Rinse the zucchini. Snip off and discard the flower stalks and grate the zucchini coarsely.
3. Mix the remaining 4 tsp/20 g salt into the grated zucchini in a bowl.
4. Pack the zucchini into the container, pressing down firmly so that any trapped air bubbles are released.
5. Cover the surface and make sure that the strips are well covered by the brine. Place a lid or plate on top and let the container stand at room temperature for 2 weeks. Check the fluid level in the container regularly; if it drops, add more boiled and cooled brine.
6. The zucchini will be ready to eat after 2 weeks and should be stored in the refrigerator.

ONIONS

Thanks to their high sugar content, onions of any kind are easy to pickle.

4 canning jars that can hold 2 cups/500 ml each
1½ quarts/1.5 liters water
6 tsp/30 g iodine-free salt
2¼ lb/1 kg onions, such as shallots, garlic or pickling onions

1. Boil the water, add the salt, and let the brine cool.
2. Peel the onions. The skins will come off more easily if you first immerse the onions in boiled water for about 30 seconds. Garlic needs to be cleaned, but not necessarily peeled.
3. Distribute the onions between the jars, pour over the brine, and close the lids.
4. Let the jars stand at room temperature for 10 days; the onions will now be ready to eat. Store in the refrigerator.

BELL PEPPERS

2-quart/2-liter container
1½ quarts/1.5 liters water
2½ tbsp/50 g iodine-free salt
3¼ lb/1.5 kg fresh bell peppers
1 onion, peeled and finely chopped
peeled garlic cloves, to taste

1. Boil the water, add the salt, and let the brine cool to room temperature.
2. Wash the bell peppers before cutting them into quarters, trimming off the area around the stalk, and removing the membranes and seeds.
3. Place the onion and garlic in the bottom of the container. Now layer the peppers on top and pour over the brine. Cover with a lid or a plate.
4. Let the container stand at room temperature for 10 days; the bell peppers will now be ready to eat. Store in the refrigerator.

CAULIFLOWER

2-quart/2-liter container
1 quart/1 liter water
1 tbsp/20 g iodine-free salt
2¼ lb/1 kg cauliflower (Romanesco variety works well)
1 onion, peeled and finely chopped

1. Boil the water, add the salt, and let the brine cool to room temperature.
2. Break the cauliflower into small, delicate florets.
3. Place the onion in the bottom of the container and add the cauliflower florets. Pour over the brine so that the cauliflower is completely covered.
4. Press the cauliflower florets down beneath the surface of the brine and cover with a lid.
5. Let the container stand at room temperature for 10–14 days, when the cauliflower will be ready to eat. Store in the refrigerator.

CHILE PEPPERS

The recipe for bell peppers can also be used for chiles; as these are so strong in flavor, you may only need a smaller amount.

17-ounce/500-ml glass container
1¼ cups/300 ml water
1½ tsp/7.5 g iodine-free salt
11 oz/300 g chiles

1. Boil the water, add the salt, and let the brine cool to room temperature.
2. Wash the chiles, then trim off the area around the stalk, and layer the chiles in the container. Pour over the brine to cover them completely and close the lid.
3. Let the container stand at room temperature for 10 days; the chiles will now be ready to eat, so store in the refrigerator.

SAUERKRAUT (LARGE BATCH)

10-quart/10-liter container (or three 3-quart/3-liter containers)
5½ tbsp/110 g iodine-free salt
17½ lb/8 kg cabbage, well cleaned, with wilted, limp leaves removed

1. Shred the cabbage extremely finely, into very thin strips. You could use a mandoline or a special kraut board. Chop the stalk finely with a special cabbage corer or tear it coarsely.
2. Layer the cabbage with the salt in a large mixing bowl. Make sure that the salt is well distributed throughout the cabbage.
3. Press down on the cabbage until all the juices and air bubbles are removed.
4. Pack the cabbage and all the juices that have come out of the cabbage into the container. Make sure that all the cabbage is covered by salty cabbage water—there should be at least ¾ inch/2 cm of clearance. If not, boil some brine, using 2 tsp/10 g salt for every quart/liter of water. Let the brine cool, then pour it over the cabbage.
5. Cover the cabbage completely by placing a couple of sturdy, well-cleaned cabbage leaves on top. Press the cabbage down beneath the surface of the liquid. You could use a tightly sealed water-filled plastic bag or the weights from your traditional ceramic pickling jar, if you are using one, or even a plate and a large stone that has been thoroughly cleaned and boiled to sterilize it (do not use limestone). Cover with a loose-fitting lid or plate.
6. Let the container stand for 2 days at 68–71.6°F/20–22°C. Check the fluid level in the container regularly; if it drops, add some more boiled and cooled brine.
7. After 2 days, move the container to a place that is about 59–64.4°F/15–18°C and store for 10–14 days (or less if the temperature is higher).
8. The sauerkraut will be ready in about 2 weeks, after which it should be stored in the refrigerator.

SAUERKRAUT (SMALL BATCH)

2-quart/2-liter canning jar
2 tbsp/40 g iodine-free salt
4½ lb/2 kg cabbage, well cleaned, with wilted, limp leaves removed

1. Trim and clean the cabbage and shred very thinly. Shred the cabbage stalks coarsely with a grater.
2. Layer the cabbage and salt in a large bowl, pressing firmly with your fists so the cabbage releases its juices.
3. Pack the cabbage and all the salty cabbage juices in the jar, pressing down hard with your fists to release any air bubbles. Make sure that all the cabbage is covered by the salty cabbage liquid.
4. Cover the mixture completely with pieces of cabbage leaf on the top. Press down on the cabbage in the jar—you could use a tightly sealed, water-filled plastic bag—and close the lid.
5. Keep the jar at room temperature (max. 71.6°F/22°C) for a day.
6. Move the jar to a room where the temperature is 59–64.4°F/15–18°C.
7. After 10–14 days, move the bowl to the refrigerator. The sauerkraut is now ready to eat, but will taste even better if matured for a further 14 days.

....

VARIATION WITH SPICES: Mix salt with 1 tsp/5 g cumin per 2¼ lb/1 kg cabbage. You can also use the same amount of coarsely ground coriander seeds. Some people like garlic cloves in their sauerkraut, others use juniper; I prefer to flavor it during the cooking process—it gives you more flexibility.

VARIATION WITH APPLES: Layer the pressed cabbage with finely sliced apple. Apples do not pickle well alone as their high acidity inhibits the bacteria, but they work well in combination with cabbage. This produces extra tart apples with a lovely texture, excellent with goose, duck, and other roasts.

VARIATION WITH RED CABBAGE: Follow the recipe for sauerkraut (small batch), but use red cabbage instead of ordinary cabbage. Shred this into slightly thicker slices. NB Red cabbage usually contains less juice than ordinary cabbage.

SARMA

In Turkey and the Balkans they often pickle the whole cabbage for a dish known as sarma. *The pickled cabbage leaves are stuffed with a ground beef filling—the forerunner of stuffed cabbage. They use a special kind of cabbage with fairly loose leaves and a flattened head, often purplish in color.*

10-quart/10-liter plastic bucket or canning jar
5 quart/5 liters water
9 tbsp/180 g iodine-free salt
11 lb/5 kg cabbage, suitable for sarma

1. Dissolve the salt in the water a few hours before you start pickling, or boil the water, add the salt, and let the brine cool to room temperature.
2. Trim and clean the cabbage heads. Prick a few holes in them with a sharp knife and place them in the bucket or canning jar.
3. Pour the brine over the cabbage, making sure they are completely covered.
4. Press the cabbage down into the brine—you could use a tightly sealed, water-filled plastic bag—and cover with a large plate or a loose-fitting lid.
5. Let the container stand at room temperature for a few days, before moving it to a room with a temperature of 59°F/15°C.
6. The sarma cabbages will be ready after about 10 days, after which time they can be stored in the refrigerator. A well-insulated container on a balcony (if you are lucky enough to have one and if the local climate is cool enough) will also do.

....

VARIATION: Alternate the whole cabbage heads with layers of shredded cabbage. Reduce the amount of water to 2 quarts/2 liters, but keep the same amount of salt as in the original recipe. If the brine does not cover the cabbage, top off with more boiled, cooled water.

KIMCHI

One day, I shall travel to Korea in search of the origins of pickled cabbage, but until then, I am happy to rely on this recipe. The basic recipe is from my colleague, Peter Sandberg, who has visited the country many times.

2-quart/2-liter glass jar
about 1 quart/1 liter water
5 tbsp/100 g iodine-free salt
1 head of napa cabbage, about 2¼ lb/1 kg
1 pear
1 large piece of ginger
1 tbsp/15 g red pepper flakes
1 tsp/5 ml Thai fish sauce
3 scallions
1 radish

1. Dissolve the salt in the water in a bowl.
2. Wash and clean the cabbage. Cut it lengthwise into two halves.
3. Place the two halves in a bowl and cover with the brine. Place a plate or something heavy on top of the cabbage to hold it under the liquid and let stand overnight.
4. Remove the cabbage from the brine and drain.
5. Peel and grate the pear and ginger, then mix with the red pepper flakes and fish sauce. Trim and wash the scallions and cut into thin slices.
   Peel the radish and grate coarsely. Mix the scallions and radish into the blended spices.
6. Spread the spice mixture onto the cabbage leaves before pressing them down into the glass jar; apply plenty of pressure, as there must be no air bubbles. Let stand for a few hours at room temperature, then place in the refrigerator.
7. The kimchi will be ready to eat in about a week.

CARROTS

Slices of pickled carrots in a dash of oil make a great salad.

2-quart/2-liter glass jar
1 quart/1 liter water
4 tsp/20 g iodine-free salt
2¼ lb/1 kg carrots

1. Boil the water, add the salt, and let the brine cool to room temperature.
2. Wash and peel the carrots, cut them into thin slices or shred coarsely, and place them in the jar. Pour over the brine, making sure the carrots are completely covered.
3. Push the carrots down into the brine—you could use a tightly sealed, water-filled plastic bag—and close the lid.
4. Let stand at room temperature for 2 weeks before transferring to the refrigerator.

VARIATION 1: Substitute rutabaga for a quarter of the carrots, peel carefully, and cut into thin slices or coarse shreds.

VARIATION 2: You can also use this recipe to pickle parsnips, celeriac, or parsley root, either on their own or in various combinations with carrots and rutabaga.

SPRING AND SUMMER TURNIPS

Early and late turnips are really the same plant, but the variety known as spring turnips tend to be smaller and more slender. Both kinds pickle well.

2-quart/2-liter canning jar
4 tsp/20 g iodine-free salt
4½ lb/2 kg turnips

1. Peel and wash the turnips, then grate coarsely.
2. Layer the turnips and salt in the canning jar, making sure that the salt is well distributed.
3. Press down on the turnips in the jar with your fists. Wait 15 minutes for the salt to soak in, then press down with your fists again.
4. Make sure the turnips are well covered in the brine. If not, boil some brine, using 2 tsp/10 g salt for every quart/liter of water. Let the brine cool to room temperature, then top off the jar.
5. Press the turnips down into the brine—you could use a tightly sealed, water-filled plastic bag—and close the lid.
6. Let stand at room temperature for 2 days.
7. Move the jar to a room with a temperature of 59–64.4°F/15–18°C and let stand for another 10 days.
8. After 10 days, store the jar in the refrigerator.

....

TIP: Pickled turnip can be added to sauerkraut when you are ready to cook it; use equal parts of pickled turnip and pickled cabbage.

RED BEETS

Pickled beets are very delicate and work well in salads and soups.

2 to 3-quart/2 to 3-liter container
4 tsp/20 g iodine-free salt
3¼ lb/1.5 kg beets
generous 1 lb/500 g cabbage or red cabbage

1. Wash and peel the beets. Grate them coarsely or cut into very thin slices. Shred the cabbage.
2. Layer the beets, cabbage, and salt in the container, making sure the salt is well mixed in.
3. Press the beets and cabbage down into the container with your fists. Wait 15 minutes for the salt to soak in, then squeeze down with your fists again.
4. Make sure the beets and cabbage are completely covered in the brine. If not, boil some brine, using 2 tsp/10 g salt for every quart/liter of water. Let the brine cool to room temperature, then top off the jar.
5. Press the beets down into the brine—you could use a tightly sealed, water-filled plastic bag—and cover with a plate or loose-fitting lid.
6. Let the jar stand at room temperature for 10–14 days. Check the fluid level in the container every day; watching for any beet-colored liquid, which may leak out. If the brine level drops, boil some more brine, let cool and top off the container.
7. Store the pickled beets in the refrigerator.

....

VARIATION: It is possible to pickle beets without adding cabbage, but the results are less predictable.

GREEN AND RED TOMATOES

Pickled red tomatoes are just so delicious—sweet and sour and a far more refined variation on ketchup. Home growers often tend to have a surplus of green tomatoes, which can also be pickled.

2 to 3-quart/2 to 3-liter container
1 quart/1 liter water
2 tbsp/40 g iodine-free salt
2¼ lb/1 kg tomatoes, green or red
peeled garlic cloves, chopped dill, chopped fennel, to taste

1. Boil the water, add the salt, and let the brine cool to room temperature.
2. Wash the tomatoes, paying particular attention to the stalks.
3. Layer the tomatoes and any garlic and herbs you may be using in the container. Pour over the brine.
4. Check that the brine completely covers the tomatoes. If it doesn't, boil more brine (1 tbsp/20 g salt per quart/liter of water), let it cool, then pour over the tomatoes.
5. Press the tomatoes down into the brine—you could use a tightly sealed, water-filled plastic bag—and cover with a lid or plate.
6. Let the container stand at room temperature for about 2 weeks, checking regularly that the tomatoes are still immersed in the brine. If the brine level drops, boil some more brine, let cool, and top off the container.
7. The pickled tomatoes will be ready to eat after 2 weeks, after which time they should be stored in the refrigerator.

....

VARIATION: You can also cut unripe, green tomatoes into pieces instead of pickling them whole. Red tomatoes and beans pickle very well in the same canning jar, ideally with some added chopped onion.

MIXED PICKLES

Mix together any vegetables you like—your own imagination and the basic requirements of lactic acid bacteria are the only limitations. Cauliflower florets, onions, cucumbers, garlic cloves, bell peppers, and tomatoes are commonly used in pickles. Season with mustard seeds, coriander seeds, or other interesting seeds.

For every 2¼ lb/1 kg cleaned vegetables:

1 quart/1 liter cooled boiled water
4 tsp/20 g iodine-free salt

1. Place the vegetables in jars.
2. Boil the water, add the salt, and let the brine cool.
3. Pour the brine into the jars, making sure that the vegetables are completely covered.
4. Push the vegetables down under the surface of the brine, and close the lids.
5. Let the jars stand at room temperature for 10–14 days, then store in the refrigerator.

SOURDOUGH BREAD WITH RYE AND BARLEY

I think this book should contain a recipe for sourdough bread, even though it requires slightly different strains of bacteria from the vegetables. Sourdough is mostly made with a lactic acid bacteria called *Lactobacillus sanfranciscensis* that lives in a fascinating symbiosis with a fungus called *Candida milleri*. When I was younger I worked for several years as a baker, and this recipe is the best I ever found. It originally came from my friend Johan Swanljung, but I have added a few things, including pearl barley: researchers at Lund University in Sweden have since shown that the pearl barley in bread stabilizes blood sugar levels for a good few hours after consumption.

EQUIPMENT: Oblong bread pan (preferably nonstick), kitchen scales, large mixing bowl, wooden spoon, plastic or rubber spatula or scraper.

INGREDIENTS:
7 oz/200 g rye sourdough starter (*see opposite*)
1⅓ cups/200 g + 2 cups/300 g + ⅔ cup/100 g coarsely ground rye flour
generous ¾ cup/200 ml + 1¼ cups/300 ml water
2 tsp/10 g iodine-free salt + 1 tbsp/15 ml water
generous ¾ cup/200 ml water + 1 cup/200 g pearl barley, if required
canola oil, for greasing

DAY 1, EVENING:
- Mix the rye sourdough starter with the 1⅓ cups/200 g rye flour and a generous ¾ cup/200 ml water. Let stand in quite a warm place overnight, ideally at 77–86°F/25–30°C.
- Mix the 2 tsp/10 g salt and 1 tbsp/15 ml of water in a small bowl.
- If you want to add the pearl barley, boil the ¾ cup/200 ml water and pour it over the barley. Let stand overnight.

DAY 2, MORNING:
- Mix the 2 cups/300 g rye flour with 1¼ cups/300 ml water and stir. Set aside 7 oz/200 g of the dough in a glass jar and store in the refrigerator for your next baking session.

- Add the salt and water mixture to the further ⅔ cup/100 g flour. Add the soaked barley if required. Combine well to make a soft dough.
- Grease the baking pan with a little oil. Transfer the dough from the bowl to the pan using a spatula. Place the pan in a warm place, ideally at 77–86°F/25–30°C.

DAY 2, AFTERNOON OR EVENING:
- When the dough looks like it has finished fermenting (when it has risen by about 50 percent), heat the oven to 375°F/190°C.
- Place the pan on a rack in the lower part of the oven and bake for 60 minutes.
- Remove the pan from the oven, turn the bread out onto a rack, then place the bread back in the oven and turn off the heat. Let the bread stand in the oven until it has cooled. Let the bread rest overnight before slicing.

SOURDOUGH

The easiest way to start a new sourdough mixture is to obtain a portion from someone who already has a sourdough culture on the go, then mix this with ⅔ cup/100g rye flour and 7 tbsp/100 ml water. If this is not possible, you can start your own culture. It is very easy but it takes 4 days:

1. Mix 3 tbsp/25 g organic rye flour and 7 tbsp/100 ml water in a large glass jar with a lid. Let stand in the dark at room temperature (or ideally at 77–86°F/25–30°C) for 3 days.
2. Stir in ½ cup/75 g organic rye flour and let stand for one day. You will now have 7 oz/200 g of sourdough that is ready to use in the bread recipe above.
3. Store the sourdough mixture in the refrigerator. If you leave more than 10 days between sourdough baking sessions, you need to feed the dough: discard 3½ oz/100 g of the old mixture and replace with 3½ tbsp/50 ml water and ⅓ cup/50 g flour. Mix and replace the jar in the refrigerator. If the mixture smells fresh and good, it will easily be able to leaven the bread.

WEIGHING SALT: To get the amounts right, it is best to weigh salt using tablespoons and teaspoons. You can also measure it by volume or using digital scales if you have access to them.

- 1 tablespoon = ¾ oz/18 g/15 ml salt (fine)

4. GREAT PICKLE DISHES

RUSSIAN COCKTAIL SNACKS WITH PICKLED CUCUMBER

The Russians knew what they were doing when they paired their pickled cucumbers with a dab of creamed honey and a little sour cream. The saltiness, sourness, sweetness, and creamy richness blend together in perfect harmony.

2 pickled cucumbers
about 2 tsp/10 g runny honey
about 2 tbsp/30 ml sour cream or crème fraîche

1. Cut the cucumbers lengthwise into eight long, narrow segments. Place a couple of segments on each plate.
2. Add a teaspoonful of honey and a little sour cream or crème fraîche to each plate.
3. Serve with a good drink.

TIP: If the honey has solidified, thin it out again by heating it in a water bath: spoon the honey into a heat-resistant jar and let it stand in a pan of boiling water until the honey has softened.

Smetana is an Eastern European version of sour cream and can be found in well-stocked dairy stores. If you can't find it, use crème fraîche as a first choice substitute and sour cream as a second.

Russians usually drink vodka with cucumbers, and then drink the cucumber pickling water the day after to soothe the hangover. I would suggest a milder beverage, perhaps a favorite beer or a wine.

ZUCCHINI SALAD WITH APPLE

The idea of pickled zucchini came to me one summer when the vegetable patch produced more than we could eat. It was an inspired notion, as we discovered to our delight a few months later. This salad needs no more than a couple of minutes to prepare and takes a range of dishes, from fried or smoked fish to smoked meats, to a whole new level.

generous ¾ cup/200 ml pickled zucchini (courgettes)
2 apples, preferably red
3½ tbsp/50 ml mayonnaise

1. Drain the zucchini in a colander for a few minutes.
2. Peel and cut the apples into small cubes.
3. Mix the zucchini, apple cubes, and mayonnaise in a bowl.
4. Serve.

HERRING SALAD

This salad is a star dish that can be enjoyed throughout the year. Serve it as a delicious appetizer, on a Swedish-style smörgåsbord, *or as a topping for an open sandwich on homemade sourdough rye bread (see page 74).*

2 salted herring fillets
1 onion
2 cold boiled potatoes, peeled
1 pickled cucumber
2 apples
2½ tbsp/40 ml pickled beets
1–2 hard-boiled eggs, to taste

1. Soak the herring fillets by placing them in a large bowl with plenty of water and letting them stand for about 10 hours.
2. Peel and finely chop the onion; dice the potatoes and cucumber.
3. Core the apples and cut into small cubes.
4. Mix all the ingredients including the beets and let stand for a few hours.
5. Garnish the herring salad with the boiled eggs. It looks particularly attractive if you chop up the yolks and whites separately and make a pattern on top of the salad.

CHOUCROUTE GARNIE

Cooked sauerkraut served with good quality sausage is a tasty winter treat, but if you want to put on a real meat feast, go for the dish known in Northern France as choucroute garnie. *There should be at least three different kinds of charcuterie or other meats, some of which should be slightly smoked or salted. These might include salt pork with crackling, pickled pork, salt beef brisket, smoked or confit of duck, and German* bratwurst *or Thuringian sausages. The wine to accompany this is usually a dry white Riesling or a spicier Gewürztraminer.*

11 oz/300 g smoked pork
1 onion, peeled and finely chopped
generous ¾ cup/200 ml dry white wine
1 bay leaf
1 garlic clove, peeled
4 black peppercorns
1 tsp/5 g whole cumin seeds
5 juniper berries
2¼ lb/1 kg sauerkraut
14 oz/400 g fine, good quality sausages, ideally lightly smoked (you can also add boiled, salted beef brisket, and smoked or confit of duck)
parsley, fresh thyme, to taste

1. Cut the pork into 2-inch/5-cm slices. Cut one of the slices into small cubes and brown these in a heavy-bottomed, ovenproof, (preferably) enameled saucepan. Reduce the heat, add the onion, and fry for a few minutes.
2. Add the wine, bay leaf, garlic, spices, juniper berries, and sauerkraut (if it has been standing for a long time, you might like to rinse it out with plenty of cold water first).
3. Bring the liquid to a boil, cover with the lid, and place in the oven at 347°F/175°C for 1¼ hours.
4. Remove the pan from the oven and add the remaining pork slices and any other cuts of meat that you wish to use. Replace the lid and return the pan to the oven for another 45 minutes.
5. Fry the sausages gently in a skillet over a low heat.
6. Remove the pan from the oven. Place the sauerkraut on a large platter and arrange the sausage and any other meat on top. Garnish with a few sprigs of thyme and chopped parsley. Et voilà!

SZEGED GOULASH

This goulash stew comes from the city of Szeged in Hungary, but it is popular throughout Central Europe. The secret lies in the paprika—one mild, one hot. Try to use Hungarian paprika if possible.

generous 1 lb/500 g pork loin or stewing pork
1 tbsp/15 g each mild paprika and hot paprika
½ tsp/2.5 g salt
a little finely ground white pepper
2 yellow onions
1 garlic clove, peeled
1 tbsp shortening, butter, or oil, or half and half of each
generous ¾ cup/200 ml water (or 7 tbsp/100 ml each water/wine), to deglaze
14 oz/400 g sauerkraut
2 tsp/10 ml sour cream or crème fraîche
dumplings, potatoes, cereals, or pasta, to serve

1. Trim the meat and cut into bite-size pieces. Mix with the paprika, salt, and pepper in a bowl and let stand for 15–30 minutes.
2. Peel and halve the onions. Cut them into slices. Mince the garlic clove.
3. Heat the fat in a skillet and brown the meat in batches, making sure not to burn the paprika powder. Transfer the browned meat to a bowl.
4. Reduce the heat to low and fry the onion and garlic for a few minutes.
5. Transfer the chopped onion to a heavy-bottomed pot with a lid. Deglaze the skillet with the water (or wine) and pour the results into the pot. Bring to a boil for a minute, stirring so that it does not catch on the bottom.
6. Add the browned meat and juices, cover, and let simmer for about 1¼ hours.
7. Add the sauerkraut and cook for another 15 minutes.
8. Season to taste if necessary—sauerkraut, salt, and paprika is a strong combination, so you may not need to add salt and pepper.
9. Serve with sour cream or crème fraîche, or your choice of dumplings, potatoes, cereals, or pasta.

TIP: For an even more colorful stew, add finely shredded red, green, and yellow bell peppers to the pot about 10 minutes before the goulash is ready.

ESTONIAN STEW

Estonia's most traditional fare is a rustic dish that is extremely easy to prepare—
the oven does almost all the work.

11 oz/300 g smoked pork
¾ cup/150 g pearl barley
generous ¾cup/200 ml water
2 cups/500 ml sauerkraut
4 small red apples
pickled cucumbers, to serve

1. Preheat the oven to 347°F/175°C.
2. Place all the ingredients except the apples in an ovenproof dish with a lid.
3. Cover the dish with the lid and place in the oven for 1 hour 40 minutes.
4. Remove the dish from the oven and add the apples, then return to the oven and cook for another 20 minutes.
5. Remove the dish again, then take out the piece of pork, trim off the rind, and cut the meat into neat disks. Place the pork slices on top of the stew and serve, ideally with pickled cucumbers.

....

TIP: If you can get hold of pickled apples, use them instead of fresh ones; they need to be heated in the pan for about 5 minutes.

BEET SALAD WITH WALNUTS

Of all the pickle dishes I have tried so far, this is my favorite. It will have pride of place on any buffet table in winter or spring, but it is also suitable as an appetizer or as an easy main course served with a little ham or fried cheese—or even as a spread on sandwiches.

generous ¾ cup/200 ml pickled beets, coarsely grated
8 walnuts
3½ tbsp/50 ml sour cream or crème fraîche
salt and white pepper
chives, to taste

1. Let the beets drain in a colander for a few minutes.
2. Coarsely chop the walnuts, checking to make sure that none are rotten.
3. Mix the beets, sour cream or crème fraîche, and walnuts in a bowl. Season with salt and white pepper, if required; it may not be necessary as the pickled beets will be quite salty already.
4. Serve, ideally sprinkled with a few finely chopped chives.

BORSCHT

1 onion
1 garlic clove, peeled
1¾ oz/50 g celeriac
1 parsnip
2 carrots
4 full-size beets
7 oz/200 g cabbage or an equivalent amount of sauerkraut
2 tbsp/30 ml canola oil or similar
2 cups/500 ml meat stock
generous ¾ cup/200 ml pickled beets with their pickling liquid
salt and white pepper

TO SERVE: sour cream or crème fraîche, diced pickled cucumber;
you can also serve the meat used to make the stock, cut into small cubes

1. Peel and chop the onion. Mince the garlic clove.
2. Peel and grate all the vegetables.
3. Fry the onion and garlic in the oil in a large, heavy-bottomed pot or
   saucepan.
4. Add the shredded celeriac, parsnip, carrots, beets, and cabbage. Add the
   stock and simmer for 30 minutes.
5. Add the pickled beets and beet pickling liquid to the soup.
6. Season with salt and pepper.
7. Serve directly from the pot with sour cream, or crème fraîche, pickled
   cucumbers, and the finely diced meat (if using), all in separate bowls.

TIP: For vegetarian borscht, replace the meat stock with vegetable or
mushroom stock. You can use water and a soup or bouillon cube, of course,
but a really nice, homemade broth improves the taste no end.

CHEESE FONDUE

In very northerly latitudes, there are not many fresh, local vegetables left by February or March, so it's time to break out the cheese fondue—a classic Swiss winter dish from the Alps with powerful cheesy flavors perfectly balanced with the sourness of colorful pickled vegetables. You can buy special fondue sets, but at a pinch you can use any kind of heavy-bottomed pot and regular forks; if the pot is enameled on the inside it will be easier to wash. You will also need a heat source (known as a rechaud*) that you can stand on the table.*

generous 1 lb/500 g cheese, preferably a mixture of strong, ripe, and milder cheeses (in the Alps they often use equal parts Gruyère, Emmental, and Vacherin)
½ garlic clove, peeled
1⅔ cups/400 ml dry white wine
1 tbsp/10 g cornstarch (cornflour) or potato flour
1 tbsp/15 ml unflavored vodka or *kirschwasser* (cherry brandy)

FOR DIPPING: bread, such as light or dark sourdough bread, pickled vegetables (such as carrots, cucumber, shallots, wild garlic stems, chiles, bell peppers, cauliflower florets), cubes of smoked ham, to taste

1. Coarsely grate the cheese or cut into small cubes.
2. Rub the bottom of the pot with the garlic clove.
3. Cut the bread and pickled vegetables into bite-size morsels. Cut the cucumber into long, thin sticks and cut the chiles into thin slices. Place the bread and pickled vegetables in bowls and arrange everything on the table.
4. Add the wine to the pan, reduce the heat, and add the cheese. Warm slowly until the cheese has melted, stirring the bottom of the pan constantly with a wooden spoon. Add the cornstarch to the vodka or brandy and stir the mixture into the cheese. Bring to a boil and move the pot to a heat source at the dinner table.
5. Let your guests dip their own pieces of bread into the melted cheese fondue and help themselves to the side dishes.

....

TIP: Accompany a fondue with a dry white wine such as a Grüner Veltliner.

5. LACTO-FERMENTATION: THE STORY SO FAR

We have been pickling food since time immemorial—probably since the dawn of agriculture, around 10,000 years ago. Lacto-fermentation has long been a method of preserving delicate produce, protecting against disease, and improving the flavor and nutritional benefits of food.

AFRICA

Lacto-fermentation is still a fundamental part of traditional cooking in Africa, the continent from which mankind originated. Many Africans derive the majority of their calories from cassava (pictured opposite), a root rich in starch that has to be pickled before consumption. This makes it more easily digestible and lowers the levels of poisonous prussic acid. A fermented gruel made from corn, durra, or millet, such as *togwa*, is a common dish in south-eastern Africa; this pickled gruel is usually the first solid food a child moves on to after breast milk and is also enjoyed by adults. Pickling the gruel means that it can be kept for longer and eaten on more occasions without having to cook it first. As a result, the children derive more nourishment while the families save on fuel, and everyone's food is more hygienic.

In West Africa, you are more likely to find thicker, porridge-like pickled grain foods such as *koki* and *ogi*, both common dishes in Ghana. Beans and other legumes are fermented in many African countries and represent an important additional source of protein to the usual grains. On the Horn of Africa (in Eritrea and Ethiopia, for example), you will often find people getting together over a plate of *injera* and a lentil stew at dinner. *Injera* is a large pancake, baked with a pickled batter made from a small, iron-rich grain known as teff.

ASIA

Fermentation is also a mainstay of food production in tropical and sub-tropical Asia, but here the preference tends to be for lactic acid bacteria combined with molds, mainly of the kind known as *Aspergillus*. Soybeans are transformed into misu, tofu, and tempeh with the help of these micro-organisms, and every region in Southeast Asia has its own variation of soy sauce, such as *shoyu, kecap, kicap,* and *kanjang*. The Chinese ferment rice to form a red yeast rice called *angkak* and the Indians use the same process to make a savory cake known as *idli* and the *dosa* pancake.

These pickled grain products from Africa and South Asia are quite similar to sourdough bread; it is mostly a question of transforming very starchy foods

into more appetizing and accessible forms. Pickling cabbage and other vegetables for the winter season is something quite different, and this technique was probably developed a little farther north, in temperate latitudes where there is a dearth of vegetables during winter. Researchers have yet to establish exactly where people first started pickling cabbage, but the evidence points toward modern-day China or Korea.

There is still a very strong tradition of pickling vegetables (kimchi) in Korea and an average Korean eats more than 3.5 oz/100 g of pickled vegetables per day—a world record by quite some margin. In the fall, city-dwellers make a pilgrimage to their relatives in the country and return with bales of long, thin napa cabbage. Only a couple of decades ago, it would have been common for households to keep clay jars of kimchi on their roofs or in the stairwells of housing blocks; nowadays there are special kimchi compartments in modern Korean refrigerators. There are of course a multitude of recipes, many of which are closely guarded family secrets. One thing they all have in common is that the kimchi is heavily seasoned with chile peppers and ginger (see recipe on page 62). Apart from this, the biochemistry of kimchi pickling is not that far removed from the European version of sauerkraut.

EUROPE

People have been fermenting olives in the Middle East and around the Mediterranean for a long time. It may have begun when olives were first cultivated, at least 8,000 years ago, but it was probably not until the 16th century that the art of pickling vegetables first came to Europe. Sauerkraut grew in popularity when it was discovered to ward off scurvy, caused by a lack of vitamin C. The Dutch were early adopters of the practice of keeping sauerkraut (*zourkool*) on board ships and British sea captain James Cook introduced it also.

The pickling of vegetables eventually declined in much of Europe; it had become cheaper and quicker to instead immerse food in large amounts of salt, or in blends of salt, vinegar, and sugar. Much of the flavor was lost, but this new technique didn't require the same level of skill. The practice of heating preserved food to kill microorganisms spread through Europe at the start of the 19th century, and by the end of the 20th century, freezers and imported foods had driven another nail into the coffin of the art of preserving vegetables.

....

Pickled garlic and garlic stems, on display in Riga's food market.

There are pockets of Europe, however, where the pickling culture lives on and even thrives. I have visited Switzerland's Chabisland, enjoyed wonderful *choucroute* not far from where the old market halls stood in Paris, and eaten borscht in Russia with a drop of *kvass*, a weak beer brewed using fermented stale rye bread that used to be sold from special tanker trucks in Soviet cities.

The Baltic states are probably where pickling flourishes most. The markets in Riga, Latvia, are housed in hangars originally built to accommodate zeppelins and one of these enormous sheds is now entirely devoted to vegetables. Sellers line up in long rows to show off their unparalleled range of pickled goods and different types of sauerkraut: the Latvians prefer cumin in theirs while the large Russian minority enjoy sauerkraut with carrots, but both groups want a sweeter version that's eaten raw in salads and a sourer one that's cooked.

USA

A wide variety of immigrant communities in America also imported their pickling traditions: those from the Mediterranean brought olives, Central and Eastern Europeans helped out with sauerkraut and pickled cucumbers, and Koreans arrived with kimchi. Vegetable pickling techniques have been enriched by other East Asian nationalities. One product developed entirely within the southern United States, however, is the fiery Tabasco sauce, made by fermenting the eponymous chile peppers.

Vegetable pickling has recently enjoyed huge rise in popularity in North America, among both foodies and leading chefs.

THE DIFFERENCE BETWEEN FERMENTING AND PICKLING

In this summary of fermented foods from different parts of the world, I have completely neglected animal products such as fermented milk, pickled fish, or fermented meats, and I have also ignored alcoholic drinks: instead of lactic acid bacteria, beers and wines are generally fermented using molds. Fungi are not the same as bacteria; they are eukaryotes—larger and more complex organisms—and are more closely related to plants, animals, and humans. Berries and fruits with a high acid content (like grapes) are more easily fermented into alcohol using molds than with lactic acid, and in any case, lacto-acid fermentation produces only very small amounts of alcohol. Chapter 6 deals with the chemistry and microbiology of pickling in more detail.

There is an amazing choice of different kinds of pickled vegetables in Riga's main market hall.

DACE
DAUDZE
Skābeti GURķi 1.50
Sālīti GURķi ar pipariem 2 l.
Sālīti GURķi ar ķiplokiem 2 l.
0.80

6. THE CHEMISTRY AND
BIOLOGY OF PICKLING

Thus far in the book I have only mentioned "lactic acid bacteria" in the broadest sense, so let's raise the bar and find out what goes on inside a lactic acid culture. A number of researchers have devoted their attentions to the chemistry and microbiology of pickling over the course of the 20th century and an extensive summary of their findings can be found in a 1969 paper by Carl Pederson and Margaret Albury of Cornell University in New York. Pederson and Albury mainly discuss sauerkraut, but the processes are much the same for other vegetables as well.

PICKLING STAGES

The pickling process can be divided into distinct stages.

Stage 1. This occurs during the first day or two, when different micro-organisms compete for the upper hand. Cabbage leaves are principally hosts to various molds and a wide range of bacteria that you really don't want in your pickling culture (including *Enterobacter*, *Klebsiella*, and *E. coli*), but there is also a tiny amount of lactic acid bacteria, including among them a bacterium called *Leuconostoc mesenteroides*. It only makes up a tiny propor-tion—less than one thousandth of a percent—of the microflora on cabbage leaves, but if you manage to keep it alive by creating a favorable environment, it will take over completely. If the culture is sufficiently free of oxygen, the salt content correct, and the temperature right, *L. mesenteroides* will reproduce more than all the other microorganisms. It is what is known as a "heterofer-mentative" bacterium, meaning that it produces lactic acid, carbon dioxide, and various other substances; if the culture is working correctly, you will see little bubbles of carbon dioxide rising to the surface during the first few days of pickling, as carbon dioxide pushes the oxygen out, improving the environ-ment for the bacteria still further.

Stage 2. After only a day or so, *L. mesenteroides* will have produced so much acid that the pH value of the culture will have sunk dramatically (from around 7 to less than 6), killing almost all the microorganisms that you want to remove from the culture. Paradoxically, this is also when *L. mesenteroides* will start to destroy itself; although it produces lactic acid, it can't survive in an environment that's too acidic. For a few days, the pickling liquid will contain an interesting blend of lactic acid-producing bacteria—a culture of *L. mesen-teroides*, on the wane, and *Lactobacillus plantarum*, now on the rise.

Stage 3. *L. plantarum*, which is better equipped to handle the acidity, will take over completely after about a week. It is a principally "homofermentative"

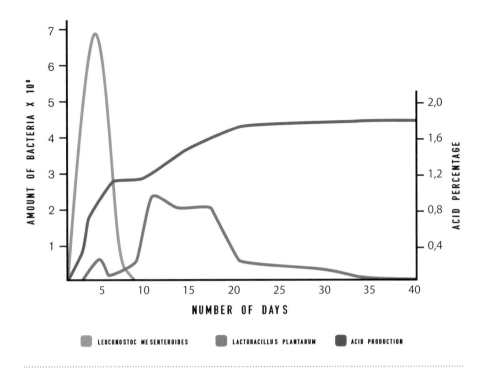

The heterofermentative bacteria that dominate in the initial phase (blue curve) of the pickling process are crucial for delicate and complex flavors. They require ideal salinity and perfect temperature conditions. Source: Pederson & Albury, 1969.

lactic acid bacterium, meaning that it produces only lactic acid, and as it flourishes, the pH will continue to fall; once it has dropped below 4.1, your sauerkraut will be ready. At this point, the lactic acid content should be at least 0.75 percent.

THE IMPORTANCE OF EACH STAGE

It is crucial that the stages described are allowed to run their course at the correct pace. If the culture is too warm or too salty, *L. plantarum* will replace *L. mesenteroides* much too quickly, resulting in a sharp, sour taste, and the sauerkraut will not keep for long. The heterofermentative bacteria that dominate during the first stages of the pickling process produce a range of by-products (including acetic acid, ethanol, mannitol, and various esters) that are essential for the development of delicate and complex flavors. Albury and Pederson recommend pickling at a temperature of around 64.4°F/18°C.

For those who are pickling on a small scale, it can be helpful to begin the pickling process at a temperature of around 68–71.6°F/20–22°C in order to jump-start the culture before moving the jars to a room with a temperature of around 59°F/15°C. Pickling can be carried out at temperatures as low as 45°F/7.5°C, but the process will take months.

NEW INSIGHTS FROM DNA TECHNOLOGY

A fermentation culture has several other interesting inhabitants in addition to *L. mesenteroides* and *L. plantarum* and we can now use new DNA technology to map these complex bacteria flora in much greater detail. A 2007 study by the American biochemist Fred Breidt and his colleagues has greatly enhanced our knowledge of sauerkraut, revealing a large range of bacteria, many of which were previously unsuspected participants: *Leuconostoc citreum, Leuconostoc argentinum, Lactobacillus paraplantarum, Lactobacillus coryniformis, Leuconostoc fallax,* and different types of *Weisella* are all present. However, as Fred Breidt himself says, it is not important to keep track of the names of all the different bacteria; all you really need to know is that heterofermentative bacteria dominate during the first stage and homofermentative bacteria dominate during the second stage. In every other respect, their biochemistry is extremely similar.

STARTER CULTURE: YES OR NO?

Almost every researcher and practitioner with whom I have corresponded while researching this book is in agreement that starter cultures are not required for vegetable pickling; they only add inconvenience and unnecessary cost. Any bacteria needed are present on the vegetables completely naturally. Much of the advice about starter cultures that is given for some recipes is incorrect and only increases the risk that fermentation will fail. It is not a good idea, for example, to pour the pickling liquid from a completed batch of vegetables into a new batch; as outlined above, the pickling process goes through certain stages and a finished batch of sauerkraut will contain mainly *L. plantarum,* while *L. mesenteroides* is required for the initial stage. Nor is it a good idea to add sour milk or whey since dairy products of this kind contain different kinds of lactic acid bacteria from the types needed for vegetable pickling. While it is possible that some traditional recipes would include whey left over from farm cheese production, it is more likely that this was because of the whey's sugar content rather than its lactic acid bacteria.

Some of the research undertaken (principally in the United States and Southeast Asia) includes attempts to find a suitable starter culture for vegetable pickling. The purpose of these investigations is primarily to develop strains of bacteria that will make it possible to lower the salinity of the cultures employed. The salt contained in the brine used by professional and large-scale producers is a problem for their local environments as their waste laces the ground with salt, eventually destroying the soil; this is less of an issue for domestic picklers.

SALT

Excessive salinity in the first stage suppresses the action of heterofermentative bacteria such as *L. mesenteroides* and this means that *L. plantarum* takes over sooner than desired, resulting in a sharper and sourer taste. A salt content of 1.5 percent is ideal, but anything between 0.5 and 3 percent is likely to work. It is best to keep to ½–¾ oz /15–22 g of salt per 2¼ lb/1 kg of cabbage. Do ensure that the salt is mixed in well with the cabbage, or you will get pockets in the culture where the salt content is either too high or too low, producing inferior results. When pickling cucumber, carrots, onions, and beans, you will be pouring brine over the vegetables; bear in mind that the culture as a whole should have a salt content of between 3 and 4.4 percent, which corresponds to 1–1½ oz/30–44 g salt per quart/liter of water. If you want to be really precise, weigh out the vegetables, salt, and water to calculate the exact amount.

As explained in Chapter 1, the salt should be iodine-free, as iodine kills bacteria. Anticaking agents are also to be avoided because they can give the culture a milky discoloration.

SUGAR

Lactic acid bacteria require sugar as a source of energy (see Chapter 1), and the sugars they crave above all others are glucose and fructose. A very ripe head of cabbage contains plenty of these types of sugar (roughly corresponding to 5 percent of the weight of the cabbage). This means that the lactic acid bacteria will flourish, as long as the cabbage is fresh enough. However, the sugar will disappear rapidly as a process known as "cellular respiration" sets in, so the cabbage should not be too old. Carrots, parsnips, onions, turnips, and rutabagas contain even higher concentrations of glucose and fructose, so they can be stored for longer without harming the process. Cucumbers have only around 2 percent sugar—only just enough for the lactic acid bacteria to thrive, so it is even more important that they are fresh and of good quality.

Beets are a different story again: they have a high sugar content, above 8 percent, but the sugar is almost exclusively sucrose (the same type of sugar compound found in domestic granulated sugar). This means that enzymes in the fermentation culture must first break down the sucrose into its glucose and fructose constituents. Such enzymes are indeed present, both in the heterofermentative bacteria and in the molds that are introduced at the start, but the process is more stable if the beets are mixed with some cabbage, as in the recipe on page 69.

Beans contain only around 1 percent sugar, which is not enough for the lactic acid bacteria to survive. You should therefore mix them with ingredients with a higher sugar content, such as onions, carrots, and parsnips. This applies doubly to mushrooms, which contain hardly any sugar at all.

If you want to be absolutely sure of the sugar content—if you're purchasing vegetables for professional pickling, for example—then a refractometer will come in very handy and can be bought for quite reasonable prices. Make sure that you buy one that can handle the range you need for pickling, i.e. 0–10 percent; some refractometers are used for honey or wine production and can only measure much higher concentrations of sugar.

ACID

If you manage to get the pH value down to below 4.1, you can be certain that any harmful bacteria that could cause sickness are gone. Only a couple of cases of people becoming ill from eating pickled vegetables have been recorded to date—one in Korea and one in Japan. Pickled vegetables are among the safest foods available.

Traditional domestic picklers and small-scale producers usually content themselves with tasting the product to test its sourness. Using an electronic pH meter is slightly more precise, but these can be very expensive, particularly for small producers. The results will in any case never be that precise, due to the buffering capacity of lactic acid bacteria.

A cheaper and simpler alternative is to keep a constant check on the acidity of the brine by a process known as "titration." It helps if you did chemistry in high school, but do try to get a knowledgeable person to assist. You can buy titration equipment from specialist suppliers for a fairly reasonable price. You will need:
- 1 × 25 ml burette with stand, or a Schilling burette
- 1 × 10 ml graduated pipette

- 1 × 200 ml or 250 ml Erlenmeyer flask
- sodium hydroxide (NaOH) 0.1 mol/l (read the safety instructions on the packaging carefully)
- phenolphthalein solution in alcohol (read the safety instructions on the packaging carefully)
- a spray bottle of distilled water, 500 ml
- safety goggles

Instructions:

1. Put on the safety goggles. Add a quantity of 25 ml sodium hydroxide to the burette. Allow any excess sodium hydroxide to run off into an overflow bowl so that the surface is exactly level with the burette's zero line. Be precise here, keeping your eyes level with the zero line so that you can really tell where the surface is.
2. Add 9 ml of your pickling liquid to the Erlenmeyer flask. Add a few drops of phenolphthalein.
3. Allow the sodium hydroxide in the burette to drop down into the Erlenmeyer flask. Ensure the solutions mix thoroughly by agitating the flask. As soon as the color in the flask goes from clear to pink, close the valve on the burette so the sodium hydroxide stops dripping.
4. Check the burette to see how much sodium hydroxide has been used, measured in milliliters. Ideally the number will be above 7.5.
5. Divide this number by 10 to give the percentage of lactic acid in your culture. It should be above 0.75 percent.

The culture will also contain some acetic acid, which is stronger, but this method assumes that only lactic acid is present. Consult the following website for information on US regulations and the evaluation and definition of potentially hazardous foods: www.fda.gov/Food/FoodScienceResearch

EU regulations stipulate an acid content of at least 0.75 percent and a maximum pH value of 4.1 percent for exports to other EU countries.

7. THE HEALTH BENEFITS OF PICKLED VEGETABLES

Eating pickled vegetables will raise your vitamin and mineral intake, help you to achieve better balanced blood sugar levels, and offer protection against diarrhea; there are also likely to be positive benefits for your intestinal flora.

VITAMIN C PRODUCTION

The idea that sauerkraut helped to protect against scurvy was recognized as early as the 18th century, and I have already mentioned British naval captain James Cook, who was honored by the Royal Society for successfully warding off the disease. He insisted that everyone on board ship ate sauerkraut. As a result, not a single member of his crew developed this terrible sickness that leads to bleeding gums, loss of teeth, and eventually death. No one at the time could have guessed that scurvy was caused by a lack of vitamin C; in fact, the vitamin was not discovered until 1936 (resulting in Nobel prizes in both medicine and chemistry in 1937).

Fresh cabbage contains large amounts of vitamin C and pickling preserves much of this, although inevitably some will be lost. The largest loss of vitamin C occurs when cabbage is boiled, so to be sure of getting the most of this vitamin from sauerkraut, eat it raw. When cooking cabbage, try to do so for as short a time as possible and using the smallest amount of water—use a steamer or a pressure cooker, if possible.

VITAMIN B12 PRODUCTION

Vitamin B12 is found mainly in animal products such as milk, meat, and eggs and is therefore difficult to come by for vegans. A few strains of lactic acid bacteria are able to produce vitamin B12, however the level of vitamin B12 present in pickled products varies and is rather low and unpredictable and I would not recommend relying on pickled vegetables for vitamin B12 intake. B12 deficiency can lead to serious symptoms such as anemia, depression, and memory loss. Those following a strict vegan diet are recommended to include in it food supplements that contain vitamin B12.

LOWERED GI VALUE

Glycemic index, or GI, is a measure of how much and how quickly a particular food can raise your blood sugar levels after a meal, an important and often underrated aspect of a food's nutritional value. Studies have shown that adopting a low GI diet as part of a healthy lifestyle may help to protect against heart and vascular disease or type 2 diabetes. Foods with a high GI include soft drinks, as well as sugary and processed foods, so limiting these products and opting for whole grain varieties or carbohydrates such as bread, pasta, and rice will help to reduce the GI of the diet. Eating moderate amounts of potatoes in general is advised, especially mealy winter potatoes. See the recipe for bread on page 74.

There is some evidence to suggest that the glycemic index value of any meal can be lowered by the addition of organic acids with food, such as those found in pickled products. In other words, eating a few pickled vegetables may help to protect against heart or vascular disease and type 2 diabetes.

ENHANCED ABSORPTION OF IRON AND OTHER MINERALS

Nearly one-third of the world's population suffers from iron deficiency, especially preschool children, pregnant women, and women of childbearing age; it results in fatigue, weakness, and impaired development of the child. Iron deficiency is the most common form of malnutrition in my own country, Sweden. Studies of sourdough bread and African fermented gruel have shown that pickling boosts the absorption of iron. The effect is largely to do with how lactic acid breaks down something called phytic acid, an inhibitor of iron uptake in the gut that is found in many whole wheat products. If phytic acid is absent, iron absorption is increased. There are even some results to suggest that foods containing living lactic acid bacteria improve the uptake of iron from a meal, and this may be due to lactic acid bacteria collecting along the intestinal wall and affecting the intestine's ability to absorb minerals. These findings may be important, as iron deficiency is a common complaint of great seriousness.

FEWER CASES OF DIARRHEA

Once the pH value of pickled food is below 4.1, it is practically impossible for bacteria that cause sickness to survive, as explained in the last chapter. Studies in Tanzania have shown that children who are given *togwa*, the traditional pickled gruel, suffer fewer bouts of infectious diarrhea and recover from them faster than other children; it should be borne in mind that in developing countries, infectious diarrhea is the main cause of death among the young. Studies from more developed countries suggest that lactic acid bacteria can protect both children and adults from the bouts of diarrhea that commonly accompany courses of antibiotic treatment.

IMPROVED INTESTINAL FLORA

Less research has been done in this area but that makes it all the more inter-esting. Our understanding of human intestinal flora has come on in leaps and bounds over the last few years, partly due to advances in DNA technol-ogy. We now realize that every human being is in fact a walking colony of bacteria and we exist in symbiosis with something like 3¼ lb/1.5 kg of bacte-ria, the majority of which live in our intestines. These intestinal bacteria are crucial for our health and well-being, not least for our immune system. The "hygiene hypothesis" put forward by scientists in the late 1980s suggests that the significant increase in allergies encountered in our society is due to the fact that we are no longer exposed to so many contagions. The immune system does not get the same opportunity to test its mettle and, as a result, becomes oversensitive, reacting to things that should be harmless, like cat hair, pollen, or nuts. In the worst-case scenario, the immune system runs riot and starts a "civil war" with the body, eventually leading to autoimmune disease. The hygiene hypothesis has since been expanded and scientists now believe that disturbances in intestinal flora could be linked to a range of conditions from intestinal complaints (such as ulcerative colitis and Crohn's disease) to multiple sclerosis, type 1 diabetes, obesity, arteriosclerosis, and certain cases of autism. DNA analyses and other tests have revealed that people suffering from these diseases often have irregular intestinal flora.

The hygiene hypothesis has given birth to an industry that touts the vir-tues of probiotics—a range of products containing lactic acid bacteria—but the scientific basis for these commodities awaits confirmation. A large study recently commissioned by the European Food Safety Authority found that there were no confirmed grounds as yet for permitting probiotic products to be advertised as promoting better health.

One approach to examining the potential health benefits of pickled vege-tables is through epidemiological studies, where scientists examine groups of people and compare those who eat a large amount of pickled foods with those who don't. Studies of this kind have shown that people living in Estonia, in Northern Europe (where they eat a lot of pickled food) suffer from far fewer allergies than those in Sweden. These studies have their limits, however, and there is always the risk that irrelevant factors may affect the outcome: people who eat pickled foods might live healthier lives in general, thus skewing the results. For this reason, randomized studies, in which scientists divide people into arbitrary groups, are an important addition to such research. So far, however, there have been very few randomized studies of lactic acid bacteria and those that have been completed have dealt mainly with diarrhea, as described above, or gastric infections in premature babies. One particular study even focused on genetically identical twins. The study looked at a certain type of yogurt that was consumed by the participants for seven weeks, during which time the scientists detected no discernible change in the intestinal flora. Running randomized studies that are large enough and of a good enough quality to be statistically significant is difficult and expensive, and the large, rich sponsors that are often required to fund them may have a vested interest in the results, such as pharmaceutical corporations or—in the case of lactic acid—large dairy companies. Pickled vegetables tend to be manufactured by small companies that can't afford such research, so if we are to gain a better understanding of the link between pickled food and health, research paid for from public funds will be required; given how common iron deficiency, allergies, and other autoimmune diseases are, this would seem to be a good use of taxpayer's dollars.

While waiting for more definite results from randomized studies, we shall have to be content with the limited observation of humans and tests conducted on animals. Scientists studying the importance of intestinal flora sometimes work with mice raised in an environment that is completely free of bacteria. Unlike all other mammals, these mice do not live in symbiosis with a large amount of intestinal bacteria and results from these studies suggest that this lack of gut flora plays a significant role in the host's life. Sven Petterson of the Karolinska Institutet hospital in Stockholm has shown that intestinal bacteria can even affect behavior: mice that completely lack intestinal flora are much more likely to take risks, for example.

There is now good evidence that intestinal bacteria may exert an influence on our immune systems, and it is also likely that they affect fat cells, blood vessels, liver, brain, and even our mental faculties. However, we are yet to establish how rapidly and to what extent lactic acid bacteria in food can alter the composition of our intestinal flora. Studies on laboratory mice suggest that any effect will not be noticeable until the second generation, and this only applies to long-term changes in diet in any case. If you are looking to influence your intestinal flora, remember also that lactic acid bacteria die as soon as you boil them, so do consider raw food instead.

For me, the fact that pickled vegetables are so tasty is already reason enough to eat them; any health benefits—either well-documented or less certain—are just a bonus.

8. TURNING PROFESSIONAL

You might be so hooked on lactic acid bacteria and pickling by now that you are thinking about taking it up professionally. You can get started on a small scale with a minimum of equipment and very little financial outlay; all you need are some homegrown vegetables from your backyard, allotment, or community garden, some salt, and several plastic buckets. Practically no other method of food production is as simple and risk-free as pickling, which makes it perfect for beginners.

SELLING YOUR PRODUCE

If you plan to sell your produce on an occasional basis, maybe at school or church, you can easily pickle in your own kitchen. You must be sure to observe basic hygiene, however; if anyone gets infected or becomes ill from eating your food (which, though extremely unlikely with pickled vegetables, is technically possible), you could be held personally responsible and financially liable.

If you intend to sell to local stores or farmers' markets, you need to contact your local or county health department to find out about permits and regulations, due to the potential risks to consumers presented by your produce. It is important to be aware of the food safety regulations, legal implications, and financial aspects of your potential business.

The local health department will want to be sure that your operation complies with their requirements for safe handling of food. The US Department of Agriculture (www.usda.gov) and US Food and Drug Administration (www.fda.gov) provide useful comprehensive information. There are similar agencies in other countries that can be researched easily online. You will need to be aware of the tax implications of your growing business, so do contact your local tax office or talk to your accountant.

It might be a good idea to go on a course in basic food hygiene that teaches the HACCP (Hazard Analysis & Critical Control Points) method. This works by systematically finding each element of risk that might be present in the production chain. One important aspect of successful lactic-acid fermentation is making sure that your pickles have reached the pH level at which dangerous bacteria die (see the section on titration and measuring pH in Chapter 6). You should also keep any stages of the process that involve soil or dirt (such as cleaning the vegetables) separate from later stages, as far as this is possible. The most basic principle of all food production is that food must never, under any circumstances, come into contact with human or animal excrement, so wash your hands repeatedly, especially after every visit to the toilet and before every new stage of production.

EQUIPMENT

Cutting, coring, salting

A traditional wooden kraut board (also known as a "cabbage plane") or mandoline with well-sharpened blades is fine for shredding a few pounds of cabbage, or even ten times that amount. The cabbage stalk can be drilled through with a manual cabbage corer or shredded with a grater, but you will probably need a machine to shred much larger quantities. It would be worth looking at equipment designed for use in industrial kitchens and deli meat counters; they can shred into strips, cut thin slices, and make small cubes, and can often be bought secondhand. If your plan is to make sauerkraut on a large scale, there are industrial cabbage shredders and corers specifically designed for the task. Machines that dispense the correct dose of salt are also available. Remember that the blades of any shredding machine must always be kept well sharpened.

Fermenting

Ordinary glass preserving jars holding a couple of quarts/liters are adequate for the small-scale professional pickler, but plastic tubs are cheaper, lighter, and more durable. You can pickle in 10-quart/liter plastic tubs, but the biological process is more stable when carried out in larger containers. The plastic must be approved for food use and do remember that although the tubs have to be well covered, the carbon dioxide must be able to escape.

Treading

I know a professional sauerkraut manufacturer in Latvia, in Northern Europe, who presses his cabbage with an enormous wooden pole and then holds the cabbage beneath the surface of the brine with huge rocks (the largest of which weighs 176 lb/80 kg). This would not be allowed under Swedish or US health and safety regulations!. In the interests of both hygiene and ergonomics, I would recommend the method I have seen used by several companies in Switzerland, where they tread the cabbage in the most literal of ways, wearing spotlessly clean boots.

Storage

The room or space in which you do your pickling must be kept at a temperature between 46.4°F/8°C and 71.6°F/22°C, with the ideal being somewhere between 59°F/15°C and 64.4°F/18°C. Most professionals in temperate climates simply pickle at whatever temperature their unheated premises happen to reach during the fall. The produce should be kept refrigerated, preferably at around 39°F/4°C, before delivery to any potential consumers.

Packaging

Some people sell pickled vegetables by weight, at farmers' markets for example, but it is more practical to sell them prepackaged. The easiest approach is to simply package a good amount—maybe 1 lb/0.5 kg—in ordinary plastic bags, but the product will then be exposed to oxygen and its shelf life thereby reduced. A better option is to use small glass jars or plastic vacuum pouches.

Secondary fermentation and pasteurization

When transferring produce from the original fermentation vessel into smaller containers, you may encounter what is known as secondary fermentation. Microorganisms that have been present in the culture (but only just surviving in the oxygen-free environment) are suddenly exposed to the air; they "wake up" as their metabolism kicks back in, producing carbon dioxide, which can cause packaging to expand and sometimes even explode. One way of avoiding this is to pasteurize the produce by heating it to 165.2°F/74°C for 15 minutes. The advantage of this is that the pickles can then be stored at room temperature for a long period and refrigeration is no longer required, the downside is that all the lactic acid bacteria will be killed. For those interested in any of the potential health benefits to be derived from living bacteria, pasteurization would make this a moot point.

LABELING REGULATIONS

Any products intended for sale must be labeled. The label should state the contents, your name and contact details, and recommendations for date of sale and consumption. You can probably work on the principle that a well-made pickled product will keep for 6 months in a refrigerator and a pasteurized one for much longer, but it is important to check the requirements and regulations with your local health department.

PICKLING PROFITS

Most readers of this book will be preserving for pleasure and will remain amateurs in the world of pickling, enjoying the cheapness of the raw materials used to make delicious produce for themselves and for family and friends. But if you wish to consider pickling on a larger scale, to market and sell your produce, it is possible to run a profitable pickling business without access to arable land of your own: the raw materials are cheap when they are in season and pickled products of good quality can command premium prices. Or you may have access to a sizable piece of land—if so, it is a good idea to grow several different varieties of cabbage (for example), in season at different times, so that you can spread out the workload over the year.

There are plenty of institutions and books offering valuable advice on starting a new business; you can research online or visit your local library for more information.

SELECT BIBLIOGRAPHY

Andersson, N & Högberg P (2009), *Sauerkraut lactic acid bacteria and their interaction with our immune system.* Lund: Department of Food Technology, Lund University.

Hutkins, RW (2006), *Microbiology and technology of fermented foods.* 1st ed. Chicago, Illinois: IFT Press.

Jõgi, R et al (1998) Atopy and allergic disorders among adults in Tartu, Estonia Compared with Uppsala, Sweden, *Clinical and Experimental Allergy: Journal of The British Society for Allergy And Clinical Immunology,* 28, 9, pp. 1072–1080.

Kingamkono, R., Sjögren, E & Svanberg, U (1999) Enteropathogenic Bacteria in fecal swabs of young children fed on lactic acid-fermented cereal gruels, *Epidemiology and Infection,* 122, pp. 23–32.

Livesey, G et al (2008) Glycemic response and health – a systematic review and meta-analysis: relations between dietary glycemic properties and health outcomes, *The American Journal Of Clinical Nutrition,* 87, 1, pp. 258–268.

McNulty, N et al (2011), The impact of a consortium of fermented milk strains on the gut microbiome of gnotobiotic mice and monozygotic twins, *Science Translational Medicine,* 3, 106, p. 106.

Pederson CS & Albury MN (1969), The Sauerkraut Fermentation, *Technical Bulletin,* 824.

Philipp, DG (2010), *Sauerkraut and other lacto-fermented vegetables produced through lactic fermentation.* Published by: Eldrimner.

Plengvidhya, V et al (2007) DNA fingerprinting of lactic acid bacteria in sauerkraut fermentation, *Applied and Environmental Microbiology,* 73, 23, pp. 7697–7702.

Pradham, K (2010) *Yield and quality of vegetables fertilized with human urine and wood ash*, Kuopio: University of Eastern Finland.

Schöneck, A (2007), Lactic acid fermentation of vegetables. 8., [updated ed.] Arboga: acidification.

Wood, B J B, (red.) (1998), *Microbiology of fermented foods*. Vol. 1 & 2. 2. ed., London: Blackie Academic & Professional.

NOTABLE PEOPLE

Fred Breidt Jr, Professor of Microbiology, US Department of Agriculture, North Carolina State University, Raleigh, North Carolina, United States.

Dusko Ehrlich, Professor of Biochemistry, Institut National de la Recherche Agronomique (Inra), Paris, France.

Mats Lindblad, microbiologist, Risk/Benefit Assessment, NFA, Uppsala, Sweden.

Sven Pettersson, Professor of Microbiology, Karolinska institutet, Stockholm, Sweden.

Gert Dieter Philipp, PhD in biochemistry, Food Tec Swiss, Hinwil, Switzerland.

Ulf Svanberg, Professor of Food Science, Chalmers University of Technology, Gothenburg, Sweden.

Crister Olsson, food biologist, Lund University, Helsingborg, Sweden.

Bo Furugren, food chemist, Lund University, Helsingborg, Sweden.

USEFUL ADDRESSES

Burpee US company selling vegetable seeds and gardening supplies. www.burpee.com

Marshalls Seeds UK suppliers of seeds. www.marshalls-seeds.co.uk

Nik. Schmitt & Sohn German company with a wide range of equipment for pickling, including clay pots, kraut boards, and cabbage corers. www.steinzeugshop.de

Steamer Trading UK company selling kitchen supplies and a range of preserving jars. www.steamer.co.uk/

Suttons Seeds UK mail order seed company. www.suttons.co.uk

TBM Maschinenbau German company selling equipment for professional sauerkraut production. www.tbm-maschinenbau.de

Williams Sonoma US company selling a wide range of kitchen utensils and pickling equipment. www.williams-sonoma.com

Consult the following websites for information on safe handling of food, relevant laws, and regulations:

The US Department of Agriculture www.usda.gov

US Food and Drug Administration www.fda.gov

The Food Standards Agency www.food.gov.uk

European Food Safety Authority www.efsa.europa.eu

RECIPE INDEX

GENERAL INDEX

(page numbers in italics refer to the recipe)

parsnips 14, 65, 113f
pasteurization 130
Pederson, Carl 108f
personal liability 126
pH levels 19, 108f,
    114f, 120, 126
    meter 114, 127
pharmaceutical
    corporations 122
phytic acid 120
picking season 14
pickled fish 104
pickled meat products
    104
pickled vegetables 34,
    103f, 114, 119F, 122,
    126, 130, 133
pickling culture 108,
    110, 113, 115
pickling jars 17, 127
plant diseases 39
plastic lids 17
potatoes 120
Prague 104
preservation methods
    28, 31
preserving jars 17, 24
pressure cooker 119
probiotics 121
professional pickling
    17f, 24, 110, 114, 126f
profitability 126, 133
prussic acid 98

R
radishes 38f
randomized studies
    121f
rechaud 94
refrigeration 19, 24, 130
    temperature 18, 130
research 110, 122
rice 98
Riga 103f
rinsing jars 19
room temperature 18,
    130
root vegetables 14, 31,
    34
rotation 39
rubber seals 17, 21
Russia 104
rutabaga 14, 31, 34,
    38f, 65, 113
rye bread 74, 104

S
salinity 18, 21, 109f,
    113
salt 14, 18f, 31, 75, 103,
    109f, 113, 126F
sarma 61, 104
sauerkraut 31, 34, 57,
    58, 103f, 108, 110,
    119, 127
sausages 34, 85
scurvy 103, 119

seasonal cycle 28
secondary fermentation
    130
seeds 38, 135
selling your produce
    126
September 28, 39
shallots 28, 31
shoyu 98
smörgåsbord 82
sodium hydroxide
    (NaOH) 114f
soil 21, 39, 113, 126
sourdough 74f
    bread 21, 74f, 98, 120
    culture 75
Southeast Asia 98, 110
soy sauce 98
soybeans 98
starch 98
starter culture 110, 113
steamers 119
stew 98
stones 17
storage 18f, 31, 130
string beans 28
sucrose 34, 114
sugar 14, 31, 58, 103,
    110, 113f, 119
    content 14, 31, 50,
    113f
summer 28f
summer squashes 28,
    38f, 49, 81

THANK YOU!

A number of people helped make this book possible. Special thanks go to:

The Eldrimner organization, who organized the study tour to Chabisland in Switzerland, where I was able to visit pickling companies both large and small. *Victoria Vestun* led the trip and also helped to research Chapter 8 on professional pickling.

Tom Olefalk and *Svante Lindqvist*, two Swedish professional picklers who also went on the trip to Switzerland and made it so much more interesting with their incisive questions and comments.

Peter Ininbergs who steered me toward the Latvian retailers and manufacturers of pickled vegetables.

The American researcher *Fred Breidt* and the Swiss food engineer *Dr Gert Dieter Philipp* who answered my avalanche of questions tirelessly.

The Swedish researchers *Bengt Björkstén, Sven Pettersson, Agnes Wold, Ulf Svanberg, Christer Olsson*, and *Bo Furugren*, who all settled any number of issues and helped out with research.

My neighborhood library, which managed to produce the most arcane foreign language books on the fermentation of food.

The NFA, which mobilized three different departments to respond to my questions.

My DN colleague *Elin Peters* who lent me a selection of fine ceramic preserving jars when they were urgently required for the photo shoot.

My friend *Daniel Olsson*, who read the text and submitted a host of wise comments.

My brother *Johan Bojs*, who investigated the minutiae of commercial pickling.

Last but not least, *Tomas Larsson*, the family's prime pickler, who has supported, encouraged, and tasted throughout and has been the best of travel companions on sauerkraut safaris across the world.

ABOUT THE AUTHOR

Karin Bojs has been involved with science at *Dagens Nyheter* for 15 years, first as science editor and then as head science editor. She was awarded an honorary doctorate from Stockholm University for her work and is a winner of both the Royal Swedish Academy of Engineering Sciences Media Award and the Swedish National Encyclopedia's Knowledge Award. She spent a number of years in professional food manufacture and is a gardening and pickling enthusiast.